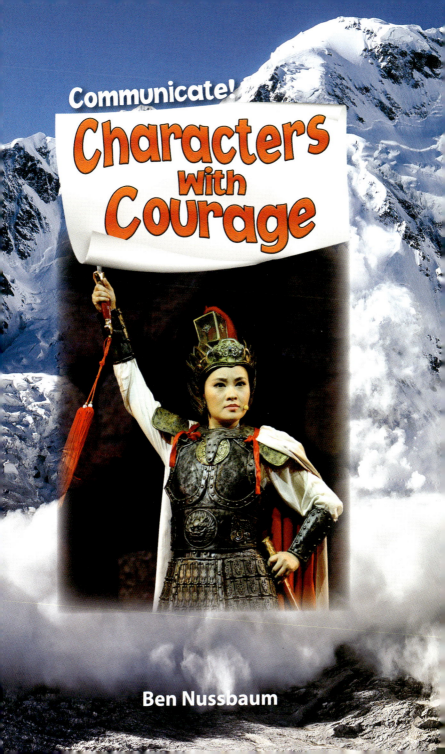

Communicate!
Characters with Courage

Ben Nussbaum

Publishing Credits

Rachelle Cracchiolo, M.S.Ed., *Publisher*
Conni Medina, M.A.Ed., *Managing Editor*
Nika Fabienke, Ed.D., *Series Developer*
June Kikuchi, *Content Director*
John Leach, *Assistant Editor*
Lee Aucoin, *Senior Graphic Designer*

TIME For Kids and the TIME For Kids logo are registered trademarks of TIME Inc. Used under license.

Image Credits: p.5 (inset) Reuters TV/Reuters/Newscom; pp.10–11, p.12 (pilot) Xinhua/Alamy Stock Photo; p.12 Alamy Stock Photo; pp.12–13 Marka/Alamy Stock Photo; p.14 Ben Gabbe/WireImage/Getty Images; pp.16–17 United Archives GmbH/Alamy Stock Photo; p.18 Pictorial Press Ltd/Alamy Stock Photo; p.20 Mary Evans Picture Library/Alamy Stock Photo; pp.22–23 Universal Pictures/Getty Images; pp.24–25 PJF Military Collection/Alamy Stock Photo; p.25 Illustration by Timothy J. Bradley; pp.26–27 Rolls Press/Popperfoto/Getty Images; all other images from iStock and/or Shutterstock.

All companies and products mentioned in this book are registered trademarks of their respective owners or developers and are used in this book strictly for editorial purposes; no commercial claim to their use is made by the author or the publisher.

Teacher Created Materials

5301 Oceanus Drive
Huntington Beach, CA 92649-1030
http://www.tcmpub.com
ISBN 978-1-4258-4980-1
© 2018 Teacher Created Materials, Inc.
Made in China
Nordica.072017.CA21700822

Table of Contents

Life or Death	4
A Resourceful Rider	6
Expect the Unexpected	10
Magical Friends	16
The Island Girl	20
Everyday Survival	26
Glossary	28
Index	29
Check It Out!	30
Try It!	31
About the Author	32

Life or Death

A family is stranded on an island. They have nothing to eat or drink. An astronaut battles an alien. A plane crashes. A few survivors wander in the wild. These fictional characters are in danger. They are fighting to survive. It is life or death.

Sometimes when people are under pressure, they show their true selves. That is one reason survival books are popular. They communicate special messages. They show how a character's best traits shine through when times are tough.

Books about survival are exciting to read. They can also be inspiring. The same things that help characters when they are desperate can help real people in day-to-day life.

Looking for a Good Book?

Hatchet, *The Sign of the Beaver*, and *Surrounded by Sharks* are great books about survival. Ask your librarian for more suggestions.

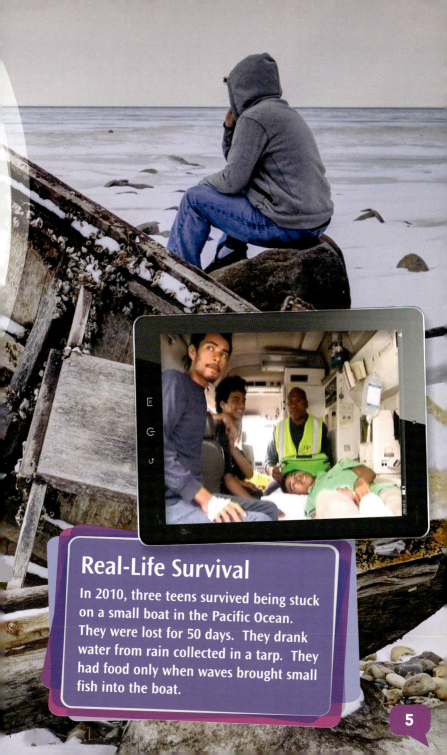

Real-Life Survival

In 2010, three teens survived being stuck on a small boat in the Pacific Ocean. They were lost for 50 days. They drank water from rain collected in a tarp. They had food only when waves brought small fish into the boat.

A Resourceful Rider

The Black Stallion, by Walter Farley, is a true classic. The book starts with a bang. A boy named Alec Ramsay is on a ship that is sinking in a storm. A wild horse is tied up in one of the ship's rooms and will drown if Alec does not help. Even though Alec is afraid that the fierce animal might kick him, he unties it. Seconds later, they plunge into the water together.

A Racer

The Black Stallion is an Arabian horse. This breed is known for its speed and **endurance**. In the book, Farley describes the horse's speed. He wrote, "like a shot from a gun, the Black broke down the beach. ...His huge strides seemed to make him fly through the air."

The boy and the horse swim for hours. The horse's instincts guide it to a small, uninhabited island. But Alec and the stallion are not safe. There is little food and no shelter. Working together, they survive until they are rescued. Back home, the stallion becomes a great racehorse.

A Long Career

Farley wrote *The Black Stallion* while he was in college. He wrote more Black Stallion books over a period of almost 50 years. Farley was in his 70s when he wrote the 21st and final book in the series!

Alec is tough, brave, and **self-reliant**. But more than anything, he is **resourceful** in the face of fear. This quality is the key to his survival. Resourceful people figure out how to do things. They experiment and **improvise**.

Alec's can-do attitude is communicated through his actions. He figures out how to start a fire by rubbing sticks together. He does not have the best tools, but he makes do with what he can find.

Sometimes, being resourceful means failing and then trying again. For example, Alec figures out a way to fish through trial and error. He uses bark to tie his pocketknife to a long stick. This spear does not work right away. He spends all day teaching himself how to use it.

The Stories Continue

Walter Farley's son Steven has continued writing the Black Stallion series. Steven's first book was *The Young Black Stallion*. He wrote the book with his father.

THINK LINK

Alec is resourceful. Being resourceful means you look for ways to solve problems or to simply get things done.

› *Resource* is in the word *resourceful*. What is a resource?

› Time can be a resource. If you did not have enough time to do all of your homework, what would you do?

› If you were stranded on an island like Alec, what resources would you need?

Expect the Unexpected

A young woman takes her father's place in the emperor's army. She pretends to be a man because the army is for men only. And she ends up becoming a great warrior. The emperor rewards her. She returns to her family.

If that sounds familiar, you have probably seen Disney's *Mulan*. The story is based on a short, very old Chinese poem. In the poem, Mulan spends 12 years as a soldier. "She goes ten thousand miles on the business of war," it says. The war is fierce. "Generals die in a hundred battles."

Mulan has a special place in Chinese culture. The legend of Mulan began in a poem. Plays, operas, art, novels, TV shows, and movies have all added details to the tale.

Flower Power

In Chinese, *mulan* is a type of flowering tree. Mulan's family name is *Hua*, which means *flower*.

opera of Mulan at a theater in China

Screen Star

Mulan Joins the Army was released in Shanghai, China, in 1939. The film became a smash hit. It launched many other movies and TV shows about Mulan.

Mulan loves her family. She is fierce and brave. But what really makes her special is her creativity. She does not do the same thing as everyone else. She has unique ideas.

One theme is the same in all Mulan stories: expect the unexpected. In the Disney movie, the enemy attacks Mulan and her fellow soldiers. Her friends are ready to die with honor. But Mulan finds a solution. She uses a cannon to start an **avalanche**. It buries the enemy army in the snow.

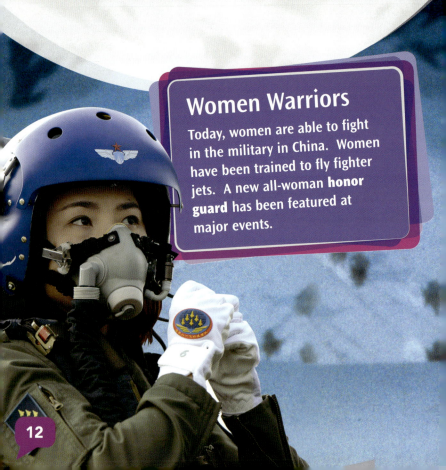

Women Warriors

Today, women are able to fight in the military in China. Women have been trained to fly fighter jets. A new all-woman **honor guard** has been featured at major events.

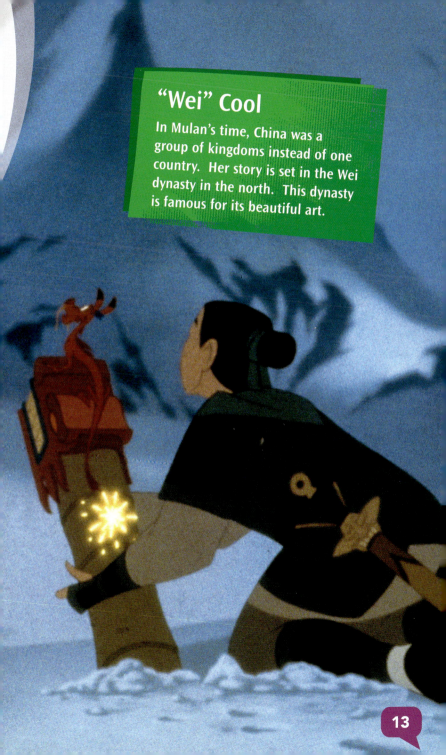

"Wei" Cool

In Mulan's time, China was a group of kingdoms instead of one country. Her story is set in the Wei dynasty in the north. This dynasty is famous for its beautiful art.

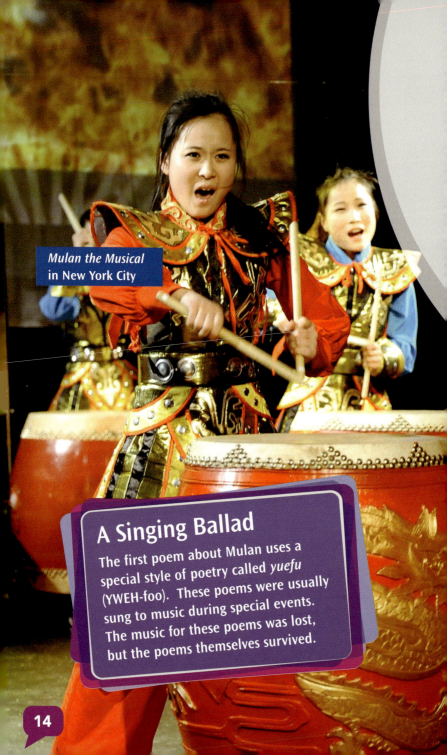

Mulan the Musical in New York City

A Singing Ballad

The first poem about Mulan uses a special style of poetry called *yuefu* (YWEH-foo). These poems were usually sung to music during special events. The music for these poems was lost, but the poems themselves survived.

Mulan is creative and decisive. Once she makes up her mind, she acts right away. When she has the idea to take her father's place in the military, she moves quickly. She does not hesitate.

Being too decisive is not always good. Sometimes, it is better to listen to what people think before you make a decision. But in the army, acting quickly is sometimes the only way to survive.

In one story, Mulan notices birds above the enemy camp at night. She realizes that this means the enemy soldiers are on the move. There is no time to wait. She orders her troops to prepare an attack. The enemy army is destroyed.

Real Mulans

By one estimate, 400 women fought as men in the American Civil War. The uniforms did not fit very well, and the armies were loosely organized. It was easy to join with a fake name.

Magical Friends

Imagine being thrown into a world of magic. You have no family. And you are in grave danger! J. K. Rowling's Harry Potter book series is about a young wizard. He must fight against the evil wizard Voldemort.

Harry is brave, skilled, and sometimes lucky. But he could never survive alone. He gets help from his friends, especially his best friends, Ron and Hermione. Even in a showdown with Voldemort, Harry thinks about his friends. In the fifth movie, he tells the dark lord, "You're the one who is weak. You will never know love or friendship."

Movie Marathon

Watching all eight Harry Potter movies in a row would take about 19 hours!

Across Generations

Harry's father was friends with Sirius Black and Remus Lupin. Both of these men look after Harry throughout the series. This is another way that J. K. Rowling shows the power of friendship.

Hermione and Ron help Harry in many ways. In the first book, the friends must overcome seven challenges to get to a powerful object called the *sorcerer's stone*.

Hermione leads the team through a large, magical plant called *devil's snare*. Ron makes sure Harry and Hermione get to the other side of a life-size game of wizard's chess. In another challenge, Hermione figures out which potion is safe to drink. Without his friends, Harry would not have made it past these obstacles.

The lesson J. K. Rowling communicates with these characters is simple but important: to have friends, you have to be a friend. Harry cares for others. This does not make him weak. It is the way he survives.

STOP! THINK...

The movie based on the first book in the series, *Harry Potter and the Sorcerer's Stone*, was a hit around the world. This bar graph shows how much money it made in the United States, Japan, and some countries in Europe. Do you think the theme of the importance of friendship would be valued all over the world?

> What do these numbers show about the movie's popularity?

> Why would some movies be more popular in certain countries?

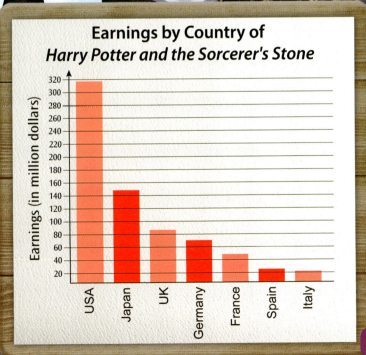

The Island Girl

Island of the Blue Dolphins, by Scott O'Dell, is about Karana. She is 12 years old at the start of the book. Her tribe lives on a small island. Hunters come to the island to gather otter **pelts**. In a fight between Karana's people and the hunters, many people in her tribe die.

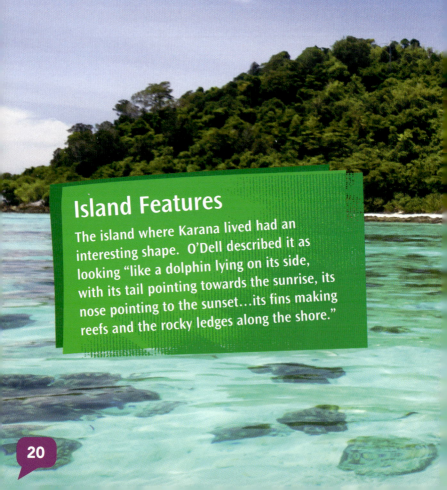

Island Features

The island where Karana lived had an interesting shape. O'Dell described it as looking "like a dolphin lying on its side, with its tail pointing towards the sunrise, its nose pointing to the sunset…its fins making reefs and the rocky ledges along the shore."

Later, a ship arrives to take Karana's tribe to the mainland. Spanish priests think the tribespeople will be safer there. As the ship departs, Karana spots her brother running toward it. She dives into the water and swims to him. Karana and her brother watch the ship sail away.

Just a few days later, wild dogs kill her brother. Karana is alone and afraid.

Island Connection

O'Dell, the author of *Island of the Blue Dolphins*, lived on Rattlesnake Island when he was a child. Today, it is called Terminal Island. It is part of Los Angeles.

Karana builds a life for herself. She makes a home and **tames** a wild dog. She even keeps two birds as pets.

Karana is **resilient**. She moves on from sadness and disappointment. She does not stay upset. Resilience is related to **optimism**. To be resilient, you have to look to the future instead of dwelling on the past.

One day, Karana tries to leave the island. But she has to return when her canoe leaks. It becomes too dangerous. She realizes she can't leave the island without help. She is also exhausted. After she sleeps for a day, she immediately sets to work making a better shelter. This is resilience in action!

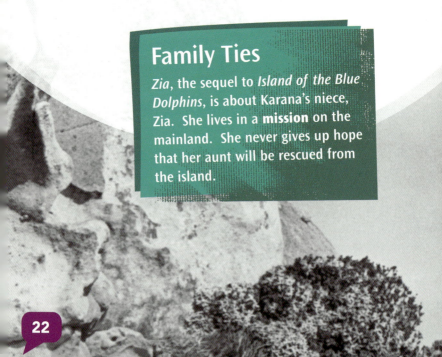

Family Ties

Zia, the sequel to *Island of the Blue Dolphins*, is about Karana's niece, Zia. She lives in a **mission** on the mainland. She never gives up hope that her aunt will be rescued from the island.

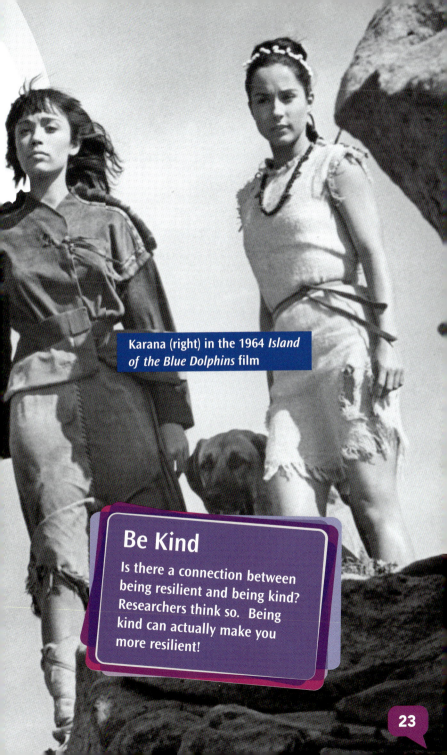

Karana (right) in the 1964 *Island of the Blue Dolphins* film

Be Kind

Is there a connection between being resilient and being kind? Researchers think so. Being kind can actually make you more resilient!

The Real Karana

Karana is based on a real person. A woman lived alone on San Nicolas Island. This small island is about 60 miles from the coast of California. She was there for 18 years before she was rescued.

No one knows what her birth name was. She was taken to the mainland in 1853 and died seven weeks later. Priests called her Juana Maria. Today, some people call her the Lone Woman of San Nicolas.

Juana Maria made water bottles out of sea grass and asphaltum, a tar-like substance that washed ashore. The island has many freshwater springs, particularly on the western side.

She sometimes camped out in simple huts around the island to be near sources of food. She was discovered here, near a hut made of whale ribs and sealskin.

Juana Maria lived in a long, narrow cave. It kept out the fierce winds from the Pacific Ocean.

The woman ate a variety of food, including dried seal fat. This required heavy chewing and wore down her teeth. She killed seals at night, using stone weapons.

George Nidever led the expedition that brought the lone woman to the mainland. He said, "She must have been about 50 years old but was still strong and active. Her face was pleasing, as she was continuously smiling."

Researchers think this is the location of the last occupied native village on the island.

The island's highest elevation is 905 feet.

In 1933, the U.S. Navy took over the island. Today, there is an airplane runway on its east side.

Juana Maria

Everyday Survival

Few people have to face survival situations like the characters in these stories, but normal life has plenty of obstacles. Pressure and stress are everywhere.

Imagine that you do not have electricity for a few days after a huge storm. How could you be resourceful to find ways to keep warm? Imagine that you move to a new school. How could you make new friends? It would help to be resilient.

Hard things happen every day! This means each day you have a chance to communicate what is special about you. Survival skills can come in handy in many situations.

Be Prepared

Does your family have an emergency kit at home and in your car? *Ready.gov* has tips for what to put in the kit.

At the Movies

Actor Tom Hanks plays an astronaut in the movie *Apollo 13*. He and two other men go on a mission to the moon, but something goes wrong. The film was a huge hit when it was released in 1995.

Glossary

avalanche—a large amount of snow sliding down a mountain

culture—the habits, behaviors, and beliefs of a people, place, or time

endurance—the ability to put up with strain or suffering

honor guard—a military group used for ceremonies and other special occasions

improvise—to act without a plan

mission—the home, church, and community of a group of Christian people

operas—plays where the words are sung and an orchestra plays the music

optimism—the quality of expecting good things and looking at the positive parts of a situation

pelts—the skin and fur of animals

resilient—tending to recover from bad events

resourceful—able to figure out solutions without having a plan or tools

self-reliant—able to take care of oneself

showdown—a fight that will settle a disagreement

tames—makes gentle

uninhabited—without any people living there

Index

Apollo 13, 27
Black Stallion, The, 6–8
Civil War, 15
creativity, 12
Farley, Steven, 8
Farley, Walter, 7–8
friendship, 16–17, 19
Hatchet, 4
Island of the Blue Dolphins, 20–23
Karana, 20–22, 24–25
Mulan, 10–15
O'Dell, Scott, 20–21
Potter, Harry, 16–19
Ramsay, Alec, 6–8
resilience, 22–23
resourcefulness, 6, 8–9, 26
Rowling, J. K., 16–18
Sign of the Beaver, The, 4
Surrounded by Sharks, 4
Wei dynasty, 13
Zia, 22

Check It Out!

Books

Farley, Walter. 1941. *The Black Stallion*. Yearling Classics.

Northrop, Michael. 2014. *Surrounded by Sharks*. Scholastic.

O'Dell, Scott. 1960. *Island of the Blue Dolphins*. Houghton Mifflin.

Paulsen, Gary. 1999. *Hatchet*. Simon & Schuster.

Rowling, J. K. 1997. *Harry Potter and the Sorcerer's Stone*. Scholastic.

Speare, Elizabeth George. 1983. *The Sign of the Beaver*. Houghton Mifflin.

Videos

Borsos, Phillip. 1995. *Far from Home: The Adventures of Yellow Dog*.

Cook, Barry, and Tony Bancroft. 1998. *Mulan*. Walt Disney Pictures.

Howard, Ron. 1995. *Apollo 13*.

Websites

Department of Homeland Security. *Ready*. www.ready.gov.

Rowling, J. K. Pottermore. www.pottermore.com.

Try It!

Being stuck on an island is a classic survival situation. It has been used in countless books, movies, and TV shows. What would you do if you were stranded on an island?

- ✗ Write a short survival story. Create a fictional character based on yourself.
- ✗ In what ways will you show readers your survival skills and traits?
- ✗ Describe how you feel. Are you afraid? Are you calm?
- ✗ Draw a map of the island. Label important locations and features.

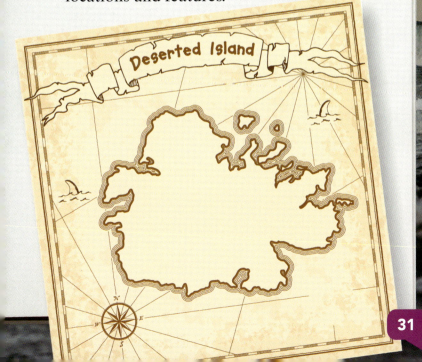

About the Author

Ben Nussbaum lives with his wife, two kids, a cat, and a red betta fish. He has written dozens of books for children. He has worked at *USA Today* and with Disney. He is now a freelance writer and editor based in Arlington, Virginia.

His favorite Black Stallion book is *The Island Stallion*. Some of his favorite nonfiction survival stories are *Into Thin Air*, *Endurance*, and *The Perfect Storm*.